THE DRIFTED STREAM:
A TRIBUTE TO CHARLES CAUSLEY

The Charles Causley Trust is an arts and literary charity based in Launceston, Cornwall, the hometown of poet Charles Causley. Through workshops, residencies, competitions, and events, we connect individuals with Charles Causley's work and legacy, as a springboard for inspiring new generations of writers and artists.

Selected Anthologies from Broken Sleep Books

CONTENTS

ISBN: 978-1-916938-70-0

The author has asserted their right to be identified as the author of this Work in accordance with the Copyright, Designs and Patents Act 1988

Cover designed by Aaron Kent

Cover art by Stan Simmons, ownership of the Charles Causley Trust

Typeset by Aaron Kent

Broken Sleep Books Ltd
PO BOX 102
Llandysul
SA44 9BG

The Drifted Stream

Edited by
Aaron Kent & Nicola Nuttall

Broken Sleep Books

INTRODUCTION

Charles Causley acknowledged the value of literary papers as a teaching tool, playing a pivotal role in establishing the Southwest Writers Collection at the University of Exeter Special Collections by depositing his own archives, and encouraging other writers to do the same.

Decades of students have poured over his notebooks in seminars, considering how his poetry, often deceptively simple in the reading, was painstakingly crafted through a process of mental labour and continual revision. His correspondence with fellow writers has also provided fertile ground for researchers focusing on both Causley himself, and on wider literary and artistic networks. As I write, exhibition panels are being erected around Exeter City Centre following a trail of correspondence between Southwest Writers, of which Causley is an integral part.

Though Causley is seen as a quintessentially Cornish poet his work has a universal element that any reader, in any time, can connect to. It also tends to raise more questions than it answers – an ideal tool for teaching and research. Through workshops, talks, and events we have used his work to inspire new writers, to discuss the impact of editing in the writing process, to analyse the connection between war and creativity, to consider the role of place and identity in poetry, and to ponder many, many more questions beside.

I am certain that Causley's published work, along with his archive, will continue to be a source of inspiration, learning, and most importantly enjoyment, for all who engage with it for many decades to come.

—Caroline Walter

FROM THE RIDGEGROVE HILL RESIDENCY ARCHIVE:
29TH JULY, 2014

> trees rain inside themselves
> the slow release of last night's storm

> one goat stands on a table another underneath
> a white horse and a black horse stare straight ahead

world bandaged in mist
muffled delayed almost unawake

> Gaza is on the news constantly
> the mist isn't mist but buildings bombed into dust and rubble

> I send prayers into the keys of the ash tree
> what else can i do to be beside them

> my feet rap some kind of pattern on the pavement
> then the sudden sweet scent of summer jasmine

HAUNTINGS

1

While looking through recently edited poems
in Causley's house on Ridgegrove Hill
a voice enters the room
and says *they're coming along nicely.*

2

What pushes through in May
is a desire to explore empty churches.
Day after day I drive around north Cornwall
looking at pew ends, kneelers, stained glass windows.
It's compulsive

and then I discover months later
that Causley called himself a *church crawler.*

3

Before applying for the residency I light a candle and ask
whether or not Mr C is up for me living in his house.

Come under my wing for a while he says
and let me help you on your way.

4

Penny Shuttle comes to visit.

Her hands hover above the keys of Causley's typewriter.

May I? she says.

Yes, I say.

I was asking Charles, she says.

The answer comes and her hands lower, touch the keys

press down. Clackety clackety clack.

5

Seeing his manuscripts

for the first time in the archive at Exeter University.

Red ink, blue ink, black ink -

the move of his hand across paper,

the breath of him

shivering in the spaces after full stops.

ANGEL HILL REIMAGINED

In war he swallowed the bitter bread
and bombs and bullets were more prevalent
than books or kind looks but even so
there was room for tenderness.
          Yes, always, the sailor said.

By day and night on the diving sea
the sailor and the poet whistled
to the sun and the moon and hitched
their love to an anchoring star.
          Yes, always, the sailor said.

And when war was over, the poet
returned to Launceston and secured
a job in a school and secretly hoped
his sweetheart might come searching.
          Yes, always, the sailor said.

I have no wife nor son, the poet said
on the day when his sailor knocked
on the door. And nor do I, the sailor said
because all I have wanted is you.
          Yes, always, the sailor said.

The poet's eye flashed like a lightning-dart
and lit up the step where the sailor stood
his heart pounding in his chest. And the poet
said, was I right to dare to wait for you?
          Yes, always, the sailor said.

As the poet smiled and turned to leave
the sailor said I'm coming with you.
And they sang as they strolled away
into a matrix of love-filled days.

      Yes, always, the sailor said.

ANGEL HILL

when shall I have my love
come to me happily
so quietly he'll remain
unknown
unless they can read the sea
breathing its brine on me
leaving no coil of his head
unspun

THE BADDEST CAT

I don't want not to see you
monk-faced at the squint window
through my blurred eyes   a leper's
through my clear eyes   a dog's
I don't want not to see you
redly   ripely   sure
as a lollipop left in a gravelled graveyard
for off-piste bees to revive themselves
the little boy who gave it up for them
blushing with none but the bee's blessing
sure   I don't want not to see you
   raw and refined
mistake azaleas for roses
where ducks on St Thomas Water
dispute and stertle   settle down
I don't want not to see you
in the solitude of Cyprus Well
where the bells of the valleys all, all
are calling Lady, Lady
I don't want not to
   oh
oh the piano yearns to join in
all that jazz of years   yields
it plays itself
sugar and cotton wool
fall from the shelf
   still
I don't want
   not
     to see you

RECLAIM THE DAY

town   your wealth is not in the dead
not between the infant teeth of dolls
not cradled in a humming spell
not a shopfront of murderer's elixirs

town   you are zigzag and sunlit
not crooked   nor bought-up   nor seaside
nor overly desirable to outsiders
but fortified   and with good bread

a profusion of music   the same skies
as lost and expensive postcodes
children and bees remixing
new stories   tell the living stones

SUMMER, LAUNCESTON
St Cuthbert Mayne

WHERE STONE RUNS ◊ LIKE

HONEY ◊ BECAUSE THE SEA ◊

IS A TYPE OF ◊ DESERT ◊

SPINE ◊ OF SELF-STRIPPING THORNS

◊ NOW BEING RUINED ◊

WARMING TO YOU ◊ I LET IN

THE ◊ LIGHT ◊ ◊ ◊ YOU ROSE

STEM ◊ LONG AGO, NEWLY ◊

DEAD AND ◊ RISEN ◊ ◊ ◊

TREASURE WHAT YOU ◊ SAY

◊ BECAUSE ◊ NOBODY'S REAL

FACE EXISTS ◊ YET ◊ POLKADOT

WOUNDS ◊ WHERE STONE ◊ RUNS

◊ LIKE HONEY ◊ ◊ ◊ ◊◊

This poem was commissioned by the Charles Causley Trust for Launceston Castle (2022). It appears in *Polkadot Wounds* (Carcanet, July 2024).

MYCRO

Hard to grasp now how impressed
we were once by this miniscule gem:
a mail-order-shipped spy micro-camera
from South Dakota – why would a mag
as banal as my father's monthly *Practical
Householder* with *hints for picket-fencing*
and bearded plywood-Santa templates
even advertise such KGB-ish gizmos?

How'd they commodity-code it
on the USPS customs form? Maybe
espionage was a regular check-box,
legitimate Cold-War hobby?

Lumbered every outing with Leica,
flashgun, canisters, cloud-filter, fish-eye,
sundry wide-angles and *Leningrada* light-meter,
the intricacy of this palm-size space-age
miracle'd dazzled him.
                    But with
folded Cyrillic instructions still crisp
inside the tan leather case, seems
he never did get to snap those
blueprints, conning towers,
the unorthodox beards and gumboots
in an October quayside bar.

HORSE

This England is So Different
— Italo Svevo, (onetime resident of Charlton Church Lane)

The huge head lies across the pavement
outside the Chinese, one large blinkered
eye unblinking, Zeno's millet-bag scattered

and the rag-and-bone cart's swag
 – a Baby Belling, telly, and a small spin dryer –
tumbled, strewn in our midsummer roadway

all down the steep hill that could crack
a noble heart. Still awesome, the head,
as those I could see inside a dark forge

en route to the tanyards daily, or snorting,
shivering, whinnying, at our fencewire
with Willie Parker insisting they loved

stroking, could sense your fear.
I'm back among cavalry
at Balaklava, Gettysburg, at Agincourt

as the totter mutters on about how he'd
be put to some great and unnecessary expense
to get the bleedin' horse shifted, and no mistake.

TIN WHISTLE

Not penny whistle, I tell the CNN
anchor, *tin whistle* – before playing
The Foggy Dew in a Kansas City Irish Fest
segment that's spiked later for more urgent
Hillary-news.
                    Always tin whistle,
since, say, the days a young
Charles Causley packed his
pre-war model in a navy knapsack
for Scapa Flow, Belfast, Freetown,

the one I played through a long summer:
found tucked away at the back
of his desk. Now in a glass case: part
of a fellow poet-musician's shelf-life.

This, on the other hand, is the one America
might have heard on CNN
from sea to shining sea, that
I've played off-air from Lubec, anyway,
to New Orleans, Carmel, Seattle,
and like the peripatetic Oliver
Goldsmith, from Marseille to Venice.

And once at a massive wedding
above Jaipur where Arup's auntie
asked for *The Salley Gardens* and then,
as always in India, told her tale of Holborn,

LSE in the thirties, then the Republic,
her husband's assassination, a Kalashnikov-ed
guard at her side for 30 years now.

You must recite us your Mr Yeats. Not
that sentimental 'Innisfree', those 'Cloths
of Heaven'. What we want is 'The ghost
of Roger Casement, knocking at the door.'

TOR
after Morwenstow by Charles Causley

Where do you come from, Tor,
inhabiting the wind and rain,
presenting your rugged face
to ramblers passing by?

Do you grow tired of solitude, Tor,
wishing you could abandon
your fixed position, join the earth,
crumble?

Do you wish your granite gleamed,
a beacon of light piercing grey skies?
Are you glad you have the weight
of centuries beneath your skin?

You have stood there, marked on maps
for years and, before maps,
you were written into memory
as landmark, guide.

When will you soften, Tor,
accept you will be weathered
over time, ground down
to a mere pebble on the land?

IT'S THE LITTLE THINGS THAT MATTER
After a display of Charles Causley's effects

A bottle of Parker's Quink, black,
permanent, not to be spilled,
a writer's tool which reminds
me of my fountain pen at school.

A silver whistle from Navy days,
HMS Destroyer, the name
of Causley's ship. A luggage label
hints at days of travel. He loved

cats, a warm welcome when he
came back. They're pictured
on matchboxes, collectable items
to keep safe. An airmail envelope

at the top of the display,
is inscribed the wrong way up
with 'T-RIBBON' in pencil
then repeated lines,

'The Quick Brown Fox Jumps
over the lazy dog!' slightly
different capital letters each time.
some sort of typewriting test.

A key, penknife, debit card,
an old pocket watch. Also
a pencil sharpener in a box
for Faber-Castell Apollo 50/95.

A miniature tin trunk, rusted,
from the Savoy Hotel, London.
A decorative owl made of felt
with a school-masterly look.

PORTRAIT OF MRS CAUSLEY

A motherly figure, she sits
in the early evening light,
a quarter-slice of cake carefully
placed upon her plate. This is
her daily ritual, a cup of tea
poured from second-best china,
the pink-flowered set.

A toasting fork lies idle,
but the sugar tongs stand ready,
suggesting she has a sweet tooth.
A bunch of anemones add colour,
though she wears black. The room's
mahogany corners give onto
a glimpse of garden at the back.

Her portrait hangs close
to his bed. Each morning
he would wake up
to its reassuring presence,
an unchanging reminder
of the love of a mother
who shared his home and life.

MEDITATIVE WALK, TREVADLOCK MANOR
February 2023

Camellias are already blooming,
daffodil buds nearly there.
The hedgerows, still dormant,
are populated by fallen leaves,
a tangle of brambles, the odd fern.

Newly planted trees create a vista
across the field. A couple of gates beckon,
then I'm on the brow of a hill,
horseshoe prints and sheep droppings,
evidence of the inhabitants at its foot.

A lone sapling, fenced, stands
proud on the slope. One day
it'll be a prominent feature, a beech
in full glory, shaped by Cornish wind.
I pick my way down to the stream.

Deep, fast-flowing, with shoals of pebbled sand,
ripple-chimes carry in the breeze.
A tyre is strung up overhead on a branch.
Come summer, children will climb and swing.
For now, it bides its time, water in the rim.

No lambs to be seen yet
but ewes with tufted brows
mill around, one dragging a bramble
in its dirty fleece. The horses
seem friendly, come up to be stroked.

Molehills pepper the land, their brown
explosions of soil tossing up worms.
Yellow gorse livens up the damp
drizzle-greyness and a bevy of brown cows
paint smudges in the distance.

WHERE HE LIVED

Silent clocks knew him well
in his house by the Well

in the parlour of blessings
where good silence

pours from china jugs with kind faces
and keeps a steadfast hold

of the bottle of Quink
and the cypress-black headband from 'The Destroyer'

and a ballad holds its breath –

the silent bird on the clock's face
is in love with the pale gold fletch

of the peacock feather lying on his desk
to show our poet's flown his earthly nest

though I still asked his permission
to cross the threshold of the house

a stone's throw
from the tumpy castle on the hill

Tunes are playing
from the poet's piano

they slip through the house
quick and neat as summer rain

as the youngling trout
in the leaf-skimmed Kensey

flowing down by Ridgeway Hill and the old quarry

WALKING THE LAUNCESTON ALPHABET

Alms-houses first,
then stroll down to watch the golfers,
daggers-drawn at Broom Park.

Then visit the Church,
most beauteous of all,
Mary Mary Magdalene.

Take heart by Dark House,
cross the Deer Park
to Dunheved Meadows and the Well.

Fair Park waits for you
and Fish Shambles.
Climb, if you must, Furze Hill.

Turn your steps towards
George Fox Close,
take some time here for quiet reflection,

Now the High Street beckons,
with teacups and scones.

Tiptoe past St Joseph's school, they
might be sitting exams.

Will you cross the Kensey?
Will you examine the Lime Pits?
Will you take a nap in grassy Lute Meadow?

Will you throw a silver sixpence
in Maiden Well, make a wish?

Northgate St sighs as you go by,
Pillory Row gives you
the shivers,

but Quarry Lane calms you down,
tells you the way
to Ridgegrove Hill

where stands
the house of the poet,
Cyprus Well of much fame.

Sibard Street has a bit of a swagger,
the Speechhouse stands tall,

the Tamar flows by,
Underdoun Dairy has all the comforts.

The Vestry is a very fine house,
and so is Wishworthy,
the wind and the rain cannot despoil them.

Westgate Street is old,
temperamental, and wise.

Finally,
X marks the spot where Sir Roger Moore
had his first cigarette.

A SESTUDE FOR CHARLES CAUSLEY

I think
they are
having a picnic
up on Parnassas,
Charles and Peter,
who made their way,
up that celestial slope
in the same year.

They left their poems
to our safe-keeping.

Each line
is fresh in their hearts.

Peter will have a beer
with his sandwich,
but Charles
will drink tea from a flask,
just the way his mother made it.

THE CREAK

like slack lime broccolis
rowed out –
on cornwall's cider belly

kale's cousin cauliflower
cream powder and pale
rugby men's ears

spreads itself dry
fractures into
miniatures of itself

the growing inflorescence
rubs and chafes
under the tension of a sudden flush

a swelling blackcap warble
popping their heads –
crunchy cabbage buds

this is the creak
sure as old doors
grumbling over the duchy

it's a far cry
from here to bishop auckland
sunday roasts

where stewed uncheesed florets
are ruined limp
the whole mouthfeel ruined –

from the first trap of it on the palate
through gummush mastication
swallowing and aftertaste

this is white curd now
soft dollops of cottage cheese
muddied by gravy

FISHING FOR COMPLIMENTS

i found it surprising
that something as posh
as fly fishing

had become popular
with chavs
so i was really taken aback

when i saw you on the riverbank
all in white adidas
looking after your kid brother

look – i don't want to get into this again
but seeing you lying back like that
in your tracksuit

made me think of you sitting
in the back of your dads
pawn shop - me

making you breakfast
and wrapping you in a st
george's flag

congratulations mate –
i like
the new haircut

especially the speedlines
shaved above
your ear

they look like
two spinheads
or scottish needle flies

THE BEAUTIFUL DEMOISELLE

eye opportunist
witness to this runabout
stretched court ship need

migration fondant
wireless micro-colonnades
damselfly funk

territory poorhouse
hatching breadth on water males
strong bollard yobs

teal letter swish skirts
the beautiful demoiselle
river linen

SNUGGLE TOOTH

the dandy lion clocks a curiosity
tiny little intrigue
mane shakes his
big yellow head with noses for roses

an intense eye
squinting for a closer look
unshaved rampant doon head
king of the flower bed

piss-a-bed passion
concentrating such passion
contemplating roots sandy pigment
silly wee figments

but proud as a petal
bares his lion's tooth
his snaggle-tooth
his by-the-way LOVE clause

THE THISTLEDOWN FAIRY

his cottony winged knowing hair
grows from internal knowledge spines
floret stems foundation his flowers

he leaves the land with a fluffy rise
from the roadside of an unknown century
late and lazy down the lane

as much a twitcher as an ornithologist
a science species of pasture dust treatises
a July of birds bobbing on a branchball

widespread legs from the leaf grey verge
as much a cricket as a thistle as a fairy
with daily dealings in skeletons and down

THE NEXT LIFE

1.   Charles Causley

My father in his crystal afterlife appeared,
and said a moment earlier he'd watched
Charles Causley wade the drifted stream.
I took his hand and gave my own account:

we never met in life, just corresponded,
but once upstairs in Cyprus Well I did
allow myself along the tunnel-corridor
that ran between his mother's bedroom

and his own. You mean, my father said,
you saw his mouth filled up with stars?
I did, I said, and heard the nightingale
singing in its twin-branched scarlet tree.

2.   Walter de la Mare

We felt the moonlight stir,
we knew he kept his word,
the question was how much
he expected to be heard.

For our part we thought not
knowing there was no word
complete enough and true
to match the sound he heard.

3.   John Ashbery

Recomposing myself after a difficult encounter
with another page by John Ashbery that proves
beyond all doubt how admiration might well not

include understanding, I am distracted on cue
by the thump of a bird against my windowpane,
a small brown object I guess must be a sparrow

until I reach ground level and discover a dead
goldcrest. After which I climb back to my desk,
turn the page, and decide what I think it meant.

CHINESE DIACRITICS OF WAR & PEACE

My grandmother learnt the best way to muzzle tragedy
was to speak only in her mother tongue.
Rěn nài was a word she liked to use
            meaning 'to wait' and 'to
            receive':
You had to embrace pain, even if it meant satiating hunger with air.
When the world war tore apart what was
            peace, she was eight, shopping with
            her mother;
the sirens never rang—
But when she stared into the
            aperture of her mother's
            scream,
it was the only sound she heard
Over & over   &   over sharper than
            flashing animal teeth,
gunshots and grenade, before her anguish stilled to a portrait.
Jiān qiáng was what her mother taught her to become alveolo-
            palatal, petaled: defiant like flower in a drought
even as the Japanese tempested through
villages, leaving only a wake of gasping mouths
to feed; even as flames of fury frothed the skies;
even as coppered bayonets rained down in squalls:
            the biblical wrath of an unseen god.
*

When rén appeared
            again, he
            was a man,

Once, stranger turned husband turned father.
Now, wilting in hospital sheets
            because the war never left
but raged silently in his liver instead.
Qiāng means gun, cancer means
bullets emptying a body. A body can
only be entered so many times
before a *chuāng* opens up
            and life escapes,
            sighing.
Liver in Chinese is always paired with bǎo bèi,
            his cold, foreign fingers entwined with
            hers,
mother tongue forgotten.
I clasp my grandmother's other hand,
            letting the warmth of her
            touch seep
into my bloodstream.

I.M. OF SARAH EVERARD

After a shaky week
         I shiver back in
News of another woman
         I swim mechanically
shoving the sea away

Memories surface
         of my own attack
36 years ago

He still swims alongside
         clambers on my legs, my head, my back
With each stroke I strike the water
         thankful for my strength that night

I've learned to swim in rough seas

GOLDEN SHOVEL: AFTER A LILLICRAP CHILCOTT AD

Even out here, there's no overlooking
the impact of second homes. The
streets of St Ives, Mousehole, Marazion, how tranquil
they are in winter. Cobbled streets talk to themselves. Waters
appear shallow; they're deeper than you think. And
I swim away from the stony strip of beach
If only all who've grown up here, people of
Cornwall, could find a home. Squalling St
Ives – Porth Ia – avoided by locals. Who truly lives in St Ives?
Others' yachts yawn in the harbour
Downalong, Upalong, every house a holiday let. And
I keep swimming the bay
but this send-up of Kernow as somewhere ideal
carries on, while Cornish key workers are forced up-country; as
so many love Cornwall, at least for a
weekend. Fields churned up for yet more holiday
homes; the best crop around. Who else can afford the rental?
Estate agents deeming a flat or a house a 'property'
means thousands on the asking price, with or
without a sea glimpse. Families turned out as
AirBnB kill the place it says it adores. A
school closes, a grocer's shuts. There's a private
school in Truro; Waitrose online. Who invented the word 'bolthole'?
Just what are we buying into? Offers
on a postcard, please. Look around
a one-bed house in St Ives, yours for £600,000.

AND IF THERE WERE NO SEA?

no shushing of the pull / no shimmer of summer / no knowledge of splash / no repetition of clouds / no clouds / no splendour of kelp / no fish / no study of scales / no silhouette of oystercatcher / the moon on repeat / no islands / no need for ships / storms would laze in their beds / no Speedos / no coastal erosion / all of us living inland / no salt / no shells / no need to row / no *Jaws* / no glamour of rock pools / nowhere for the sun to swim / no rivers / rain unknown / no place to drown

GOLDEN SHOVEL: AFTER IRIS MURDOCH

The sea is something that happens to you. An mor. An mor. This
is what I've learned as I rush each morning
like a penitent – diarghen – before a decent shrine. I
cannot – ha ny vynnav vy – help myself. I know this is simply
stated – forgive me – words mean so little since I dived
at high tide, every pore, every follicle, alert. It goes deep
this affair. They say I was dunked in the water
at three days old. I've never dried myself off
never wanted terra firma – the
sensible, the understood. That isn't living. The sea rocks
me awake, like sex; good sex, is the nearest
to swimming on a chill, bright day, out to
the far west – further. An mor. You'll say I'm bragging but this is the
place to swim – to be freed, away from the house
– its reminders of being settled, where
you find all the oughts and shoulds, those horrid visitors. They
– their commanding voices – can't be heard as I descend
into angorlanows, its bleak welcome, its byrl, one I almost
understand, am warmed by, despite its sheer
fall into nothingness out past the rocks. Yet
this neuvya – this swimming – still terrifies with
the light unable to filter through the folds
of cold, into the deep of under, how it blends, forms, reforms. And
darkness gathers like a shoal; where ledges
of pale granite glitter-shout. They are enough
to stop me sirening up, to
the known – aswonnys. Who wouldn't make
every effort to stay? Yes, this is an obsession, a
glorious reacquaintance – kales – precarious
at best. I plunge from the rough-cut stairway

RIDGEGROVE HILL
Launceston, 8 March 2023

Gravity is taking what it's owed today.
Water leaps like a hymn
from the green verges
and gives itself, gladly,
to the hill.

The clouds, too, of course,
and that thin layer of soil
not pledged to serve
the roots, nor stowed within
the chancel of the worms.

The road is a chant
only water has words for.
But I feel it;
       I have to brace my knees
to keep from joining.
The hill is steep,
and the water is determined.

Inside, dry in Charles's easy chair,
I doze. I do not dream of falling.
I do not dream of being robed
in dirty white, of being laced
with stars of water-air,
one of the welter of
silver offerings,
far below.

That is not for me to know.

GREEN MAN
Inspired by 'Green Man in the Garden' by Charles Causley

Green Man in the woodland,
his face held in the trees:
a brow of bark and heartwood,
breath and speech of leaves.

Green Man on my balcony,
dancing through the pots,
coaxing out the new growth
and tangling it in knots.

Green Man in the city streets,
stones across his back,
wriggling out and leaping
through every tiny crack.

Green Man in our shared past,
carved into the walls.
Found around the wide world,
watching over all.

Green Man in the memories
of people as they roam,
carrying the heartwood
of where they first called *home*.

Green Man in the green dreams
of astronauts in space.
Amidst the high and cold stars,
they see his earthy face.

Green Man in our future,
call him when you can.
It helps to speak the leaf-tongue.
Green Man, Green Man.

THE SEEDLING RAISES ITS SHY GREEN ARM TO ASK A FEW QUESTIONS OF THE SUN

Did you know I was born in the soil?
Did you see me fall from the tree?
Why do we need it, the air?
Are those armfuls of rays for me?

Can I fill up my roots with water?
Can I talk to the trees nearby?
Is it hard to learn about winter?
Do you think I'll grow that high?

Where do you go in the evening?
Do the others ask questions too?
Will you always be here to answer?
Or how will I know what to do?

ROUTINES

'Our children won't ever be accepted as Koreans',
says Jo. 'That's why we might not stay much longer.
It doesn't matter how well you speak the language:
If you don't *look* Korean' – she waves a hand round her face –

'you're not.' They've got one child, a cutesy blonde squiggle
of massive darting eyes and burpy pukey dribbles,
safe in her playpen jail, patting a plastic mobile
that jingles, jingles, jingles. 'But Jon couldn't get

a job as a prof in the States, so maybe this is us.
And it's good here.' She pauses, then makes the boast
affirming this life: 'Check out our view!' Six floors
below, a highway plays its reel of cars,

and opposite, other storage units of employees
rise from an erstwhile breeding ground for waders,
now pushed north. We're all playing life in defence;
they want their folks in Phoenix to envy this Phoenix.

'And I'm not sure we'd fit in back home these days',
she adds, to test my complicity. 'Coffee?' That
sounds good. 'Honey?' – Honey turns from the cot,
stands – 'Does this say "decaf"?' The baby giggles.

ICN TO LHR

'Keep the reunified Korea in your heart'
an old man had said, palming his chest. And
okay, I do. And there it stays, doing nothing

as flight KE 907 to London lifts
from a (re)claimed island, over (re)claimed islands
stacked with containers: a concreted sarcophagus,

the memorial to Operation Chromite,
which has no other memorial. A child beside me
pulls down her mask, is chastened, frumps.

'We're progress', he had added. See it down there,
a phosphoresced capital washing round its hills,
a land of neon chaebols and kimchi jars

where new friends complete the circuits
of their lives for Samsung, Lotte, Hyundai,
as I complete this circuit for Hanjin.

See the sea ooze the yellow they don't call it
here – there – with silt from China, as we skirt
North Korean airspace. *This land is your land*

I hum before noticing. Far towns are like colonies
of barnacles; dark fishing vessels ply
what looks turbid. And when we start to cross

the safety of China, from where this – that –
is ordained, a city (Shenyang?) shifts,
a molten web in new dark. But soon there is

nothing but black, the dark familiar nowhere,
and then the grind of lowering, the misted plots
of ruined nametagged earth around our lives.

MY FRIENDS THE COMMUNISTS

i. Loughborough

Timmy pedals his trike about the lawn
with all his tiny might, tips in a bed
of roses. Mummy's up before the lad
has registered the shock, and here it is,
but there she is. Excited, Leon yawns
and wags his tail – thump-thump – then rests his head
back across his paws. But where is dad?
Ah! Here he comes, with beers, buns, sausages.
He grinds the drum grill open, twists a knob,
and flamelets pucker. 'You want one of these?'
He holds a can – I nod – then sits a while,
then passes it. 'Congrats, mate, on the job.'
He means that. Deckchairs ripple in the breeze,
then mummy fills one, waves to Timmy, smiles.

ii. Berat

An old man sips pastis with Ismail Kadare
in... Paris, right? Some panelled brasserie.
'Yes, all those things', says Mirel. 'The other man, this' –
he prods, wobbles the frame, and steadies it –
'he is my father. The picture was taken the day
they met again in 1993,
the first time in twelve years. My father missed
my childhood: he said we'd too little to eat,
someone informed, and then....' He locks my gaze
which drags free, flits across his little shop
of sloughed off heirlooms: old coins, chairs, a chest,
uniforms, tobacco tins and trays
from some lost workshop, and – I pick it up –
the Enver bust I'll buy my friends, in jest.

THE LINCOLN IMP
a Lincolnshire folk tale, redux

The Devil was bored in his burrow one day
    and, wanting to watch a farce,
he swallowed an imp and blew him to England,
    out through the Devil's Arse

(that's a cave, look it up), then he sat back and watched
    while the imp surveyed all England's North.
'It's quite knackered already', he thought. 'What to do?'
    But he still gave it all he was worth.

First he chopped down some trees for a railway line
    but made sure the line never came,
then he raced coast to coast ripping down a Red Wall,
    then he touched all the moors with a flame,

then he cursed half the factories – those that were left –
    in Billingham, Barnsley, Bolton,
and places like that, until they shut down,
    then he made sure the Tories still won.

And he saw what he'd made and he saw it was good,
    but he wanted to see somewhere pretty,
so a Devil-sent wind sped him down to the Minster
    at Lincoln. 'Now, wait here for me',

he said to the wind as he hopped in a gutter
    somewhere above the south aisle,
then he swung through a window and perched on a cross
    and gazed down the nave for a while.

He couldn't see any old men of the cloth
    but the tills at the front were all ringing,
and tourists were frowning and pointing at stuff.
    Then some kids in the choir started singing

so he covered his ears and whipped through a door
    to the cloister, straight into a gran
who trudged through the caff there, teapot and cakes
    in her blobby little hands,

so he cursed them to taste like old boot-soles and dishcloths
    and made all the prices go up
well beyond reason, then snuck to her table
    and widdled a bit in her cup.

Then he flew through the church – up the transept, the nave –
    and swooped to the shop. It was frightening:
a thousand or more resin models of him
    glared from shelves, so he left quick as lightning

and soared to a perch at the back of the church
    to ponder a while on his own,
but an angel was trying to kip on the altar,
    saw him, and turned him to stone.

And there he still stands, holding his leg
    and grinning (an imp, when in thought,
will do that). Beelzebub took his loss well:
    he went to the Minster shop, bought

a few hundred more, dressed like a Yank tourist,
    then stopped for three cakes and a brew.
And the wind is still waiting there, robbing folk's hats,
    their scarves, their wits, and their screw.

MORALITY PLAY

Again, he leaves her little flat in town
and motors up the boulevard at midnight,
never lonelier, through rows of plane trees,
their heavy lower leaves full of streetlight
and roiling overhead. Then, home, his key
stutters through the lock, nudges the door
ajar – and there's a note: 'I've let you down.
I've left. We can't go through this anymore'.

It's six months since he told Jo he's 'not happy' –
not meaning it, or knowing what he meant –
as she sunk to his chest, apologised
for all the times she hadn't thought misspent,
that they had not misspent. Christ, the surprise:
to find your life now governed by an action
you'd never thought to take. And silently,
he'd smelled her, thought of chemical reactions...

His phone lights up three times: 'I feel alone';
'You werent yrself tonite babe what was wrong?';
'Well be together soon'. He runs upstairs:
Jo's toothbrush isn't there, her rucksack's gone,
but nothing else has changed. Some of her hairs
strew her pillow. Where *is* she? Her mum's,
he thinks, then calls. It rings to answerphone.

So he texts a quick reply: 'Babe, can I come...?'

PROPERTY LINE

at Charles's desk with
he's not forgotten that
we want a second home
but at least it's not just
a single-storey block of flats
on Launceston's maze of
school-stained wood
in my case to the man
of the whole room
so this is why I'm here
the light is fading
time to rest
time to rest
and go on to have a son
I'd go to bed
I'd wake only
if the world chooses to end
who will know the value
of childishness
I see it in all its detail
still very much alive
the sun comes up
with a dancer in the core
and a poem whose first line is
'They are waiting'
the poet would have seen
the leaves like butterflies
of the old stone of the church itself

he was too busy to write
of poetry as a poet
to be never heard of
or a little more than a week later
that's how it will be
for a change
from the beginning of a dream
the world would have to be told
and for the future

THE WORD JUGGLER
For Charles Causley on his Seventieth

There's a statue of Mary Magdalene
Outside a church in Launceston
And whenever the poet goes walking by
The saint sits up, and with a grin lets fly

a pebble. An ancient custom in reverse.
A playful tease to please the man
Who many love but few can match.
A word juggler who never misses a catch.

Making magic and music wherever he goes,
He sits at the foot of England and tickles its toes.

IN SIBARD'S WELL

I have spread my mat
across your mother's carpet
promising myself a daily practice;

I have come down
stairs so narrow I might emerge
below deck as you tap out Naval codes.

Your *Collected Poems*
are propped up against the desk:
you are with your parents, or rather,
you can see them in the distance—

they are still young,
picnicking somewhere beyond Eden Rock—
they are beckoning you towards them.

I follow you down the slate steps
into the September sun.

OLYMPIA

You look down from the shelves,
a photograph in black and white—

looking up from this table
sifting through manuscripts—

Hughes to your right hand, Heaney
to your left. I sit where you sat—

sifting through sheets in search
of your signature. Is it true

you were afraid of the sea?
When it gets dark, I find myself

afraid of you. I sweep your work
back to the source, to the cold

of the carriage return, to the slap
of the keys against the ribbon

as I push each letter back
to Olympia. You look down

from above as I punch
out the weight of each word.

We workshop well
into the night.

THE ARCHBISHOP
for a famous critic

O do not disturb the Archbishop,
Asleep in his ivory chair.
You must send all the workers away,
Though the church is in need of repair.

His Reverence is tired from preaching
To the halt, and the lame, and the blind.
Their spiritual needs are unsubtle,
Their notions of God unrefined.

The Lord washed the feet of His servants.
"The first shall be last," He advised.
The Archbishop's edition of Matthew
Has that troublesome passage revised.

The Archbishop declines to wear glasses,
So his sense of the world grows dim.
He thinks that the crowds at Masses
Have gathered in honor of him.

In the crypt of the limestone cathedral
A friar recopies St. Mark,
A nun serves stew to a novice,
A choirboy sobs in the dark.

While high in the chancery office
His Reverence studies the glass,
Wondering which of his vestments
Would look best at Palm Sunday Mass.

The saints in their weather-stained niches
Weep as the Vespers are read,
And the beggars sleep on the church steps,
And the orphans retire unfed.

On Easter the Lord is arisen
While the Archbishop breakfasts in bed,
And the humble shall find resurrection,
And the dead shall lie down with the dead.

BELOW ANGEL HILL
from a draft memoir

That evening after the festival reading with Jim Causley I returned to Cyprus Well, but could not sleep, not with what I imagined was Charles's agitated spirit a few feet away across the landing, longing to cross back over into the ~~corporal~~ world to have a chat. I got up half way through the night, dressed, and rummaged downstairs for something to read.

At the time the cottage contained only a handful of books. Most of Charles collection had been donated to Exeter University along with his manuscripts as part of his archive. I believe some books and photocopies of manuscripts were returned to the cottage, though at the time, except for the draft of a poem framed on the bedroom wall, the cottage was bare of anything that might have revealed its owner's stature.

Among the half dozen yellowing hardbacks on a downstairs shelf were two anthologies of poems that had been written over half a century before. Wondering what was being written in those long gone days, I flicked through one of the anthologies only to find myself staring at a poem of my own that I'd forgotten. It had been written when I was seventeen. Scanning the book's contents page I realised I was the only contributor still living. It was an epiphany of kinds. I'd opened it deluding myself I was scanning the work of long dead writers, only to find myself amongst them.

I spent the rest of the night sitting at a table in the small extension overlooking the back garden writing what later became a poem I called *Below Angel Hill.* It might need some explanation.

Angel Hill is the name of the steep lane above Charles's cottage and Cyprus Well, to Charles's eternal disappointment, is on the far less poetically named Ridgegrove Hill. But as Angel Hill a far more evocative, that became the title of one of Charles's most enigmatic poems.

During the second world war Charles had enlisted in the navy and was stationed in Scapa Flow, the UK's main naval base, and many of his early poems express the intensity of that time. Angel Hill, written long after those days, is about a sailor who knocks on the narrator's door and reminds him that during the war they'd *"dressed each others wounds and vowed our stars should be as one."* Now the war is long over and tired of his wanderings the sailor has come to share his life with the poem's narrator. Every verse in the poem ends with the sailor being rejected with the refrain, "No, never," said I. The poem begs the questions, Is the sailor a ghost, is the poem in any way autobiographic, and if so why has the narrator, presumably Charles, closed his heart to his visitor?"

My poem came about partly because after the poetry reading that evening I'd been cornered by someone who was writing a thesis about Charles's life and work and wanted to know if Charles was gay. I said I had no idea and walked away.

I'd known Charles since I was nineteen, when he and Ted Hughes had awarded me an arts council grant to finish writing my first collection, Little Johnny's Confession. Charles was private, diffident, and he'd never married. He had lived in Cyprus Well looking after his mother for many years, a commitment that no doubt limited the life he might have lived, but he was seldom the subject of his own emotional life. The poem I wrote that night was called, *Below Angel Hill.*

When those who knew you best
But did not pry into your life have gone
Tomorrow's biographers will come to investigate

A heart too private to be seen to be broken,
And to attempt the impossible:
To unearth those things left unspoken
By the poems that waited patiently on the edge
Of what you never found a way to say,
Or that you said to yourself alone at night,
When Cyprus Well rocked far out at sea
And early desires crackled like loose connections in the soul,
And up on Angel Hill
The ghosts of friendships long rebuked waited still,
And all the different lives you might have lived
Lay shipwrecked in the cluttered dark.

POET'S CHAIR

I sat in the poet's chair today,
I read his verse and drank his tea
and wondered if in his words I may
detect the rhythms of the sea,

or better still, the golden glow
of sunshine on the timeless waves,
a naming what we dare not know
not knowing, even, to be brave.

I wondered if I heard him speak,
his thoughts so present in this air.
My friend, what is it that you seek?

And as I went on sitting there,
not all that certain of my case,
I felt his fingers touch my face.

TWO DOORS

I like that second door.
It makes you hesitate, and bide
some time to wipe your feet
before you step inside,

where silence is magnificent
and peacefulness is true,
where memories anticipate
their love affair with you.

The books cannot stop smiling,
the pen can hardly wait,
the table seems to wonder:
'Why have you come so late?'

For you must start beguiling
the paper with your tale,
the words with sacred potion —
a truth to be unveiled.

PRIVATE AUDEN

If Auden had gone into the army, we'd have lost the bloody war
— Charles Causley

Some people need to be conscripted
into another army, where flat feet
are mandatory, and short sight, and not
knowing right from left; where, when reveille
sounds, you are expected to turn over
for a couple more dreams, where the mud builds up
on boots and the rust on guns. Your orders are,
trip over your weapons, hold the map
upside down. Don't win: it kills you.

Or, of course, join up. Sweat in the hold,
soak on the deck. Steady your shaking eyes
and slipping hands to read the signals,
tap the percussion someone will translate
into a story, into a torch song, Watch and listen
while your neighbour drowns in the next
steel can. Sit in that company so
that someone else will win, mark up
the maps for them. Survive; and it will kill you.

When the signs line up for decoding,
when, under the sea, the lights begin
to blink as a shape swims or burrows
fast at the steel skin, someone will need
to be there with flat feet and rust,
a foreigner in war, and someone too
whose skin has felt the sweat, someone

to recognize the draught when the neighbour
Vanishes. The spared lives signal, not quite
in synch, listening for an alphabet longer
than death's sentences, Co(n)scripted. Joining up.

UNTITLED (ELEMENTAL)

Moominmamma is the breeze

her glasses
floral headband

Moomin keeps

her apron strings
striped like candy

how he wanted her
    longed for her

her name in gold-foil
a solitary noun (no verb)
encased

all her process lost

THE FIRST FALL

Snorkmaiden and Moominmamma
bring the wasp-marked windfall
in from the garden.

> Moominmamma thinks it kinder
> to wait till the apples leave
> the tree of their own accord.

She breaks open the red flesh and
Snorkmaiden peers at the cupped

> reveal of white core, brown studded
> pips;

Moominpapa's voice can be heard
walking the long lines of rose bushes,

> the two women then knew
> the promise of renewal

CHARLES CAUSLEY

As I went down the Zig Zag
The clock striking one,
I saw a man cooking an egg in the sun

It was September 2022 and I was making my way down the zig zag path built in 1865 to connect the town on top of the hill topped by Launceston Castle with the railway at the bottom. It is quite hard work climbing up the path and you can imagine children up and down the path reciting Causley's poem where each turn in the path corresponds with an hour on the clock. It really helped me to see how in tune the school master was with children and how clever he used this understanding in a seriously unsettling poem like

Timothy Winters has bloody feet
And he lives in a house on Suez Street
He sleeps in a sack on the kitchen floor
And they say there aren't boys like him anymore

Much of the day was spent talking to the novelist Patrick Gale in Cyprus Well the house where Charles lived for 50 years. Patrick is a great admirer of Causley's work and has written a novel about him called Mother's Boy which is much about Causley's time in the Royal Navy during the Second World War and how intensely the tragic experiences of serving on destroyer on convey duty in the Mediterranean affected him. Patrick made much of how small the room was where Causley wrote his poems. I find it fascinating to visit the writing places of famous authors. I particularly remember the shed overlooking the Taff estuary where Dylan Thomas wrote much of his work, including *Under Milk Wood*. Complete with a couple of empty Woodbine cigarette packets, it always drives home to me the power of the imagination in the most mundane of settings like Causley's small upstairs room.

More than anything, I feel so privileged to have been able to wander around Launceston with a film crew picking up pieces of Causley's life which appeared in his poems. The Church of St Mary Magdalene and the poem 'Mary, Mary Magdalene' again with children in mind, a poem about throwing a pebble into a bas-relief of St Mary Magdalene on the outside wall of the church and making a Christmas wish if it stays there (which it didn't for me!).

I was very lucky too to film with a great friend of Causley's, Arthur Wills who had known him since he was eight. I asked him why Charles had stayed in Launceston all his life even though he was so internationally famous. "His roots were here", he said. "There is something about Launceston which you can't describe - there's a warmth, a friendliness and that's what kept him here."

Standing by Charles' grave at St Thomas' Churchyard and quoting from 'Eden Rock', his grave, like John Betjeman's at St Enodoc's Church, absolutely simple, just says "Charles Causley 1917 – 2003 Poet". For me that poem about his parents waiting for him in heaven has particular resonance, because not only are his parents there, but his father's Terrier called Jack which he describes as "trembling at his feet". I recall my own Jack Russell Chalky doing a lot of trembling too. Like all his poetry it has a simple clarity. It is supposing his parents in heaven but it's powerfully nostalgic for a time when they were young and before his father had died at home from his wounds in the First World War when Charles was just seven. It's the simple details that work so well. His father's Irish tweed suit and his mother's "sprigged dress drawn at the waist" - I think poetry is always about those simple details.

GATHERING WORDS AND PERMISSION
  | *after Charles Causley* |

where the river is thin[1] / high above St Thomas Water / your two hands rest / on the back / of the chair / where I sit / at your desk / overlooking the garden / your fingers gently / nudging my shoulder

gathering words / and *fine sticks of sentences*[2] / I find my voice / through yours / a nearness held / in every room / hands me the verse / with an affable smile / beckoning me on

I had not thought it would be like this[3] / you parenting my poetry / you whispering words / surrounded by umbrellas / doorhandles and vinyl / each holding you here / remembering your touch

the sun winks a gilt eye[4] / scattering shadows / in your study / at the back of the house / next to mother's sitting room / from sonata to sonnet / your imprint on piano / and typewriter keys

---

1. St Thomas Water
2. Kelly Wood
3. Eden Rock
4. Walking

MORWENSTOW
  | *after Charles Causley* |

In my driftwood hut I sit opium-fuelled
against the blowing gale and cumbrous skies
sea birds scream storm lit
in salted formation amongst
spent timbers and indifferent weed
wreckers stalk the sea's edge
searching for spoil and the living
they pull both from the surf
sailors buoyant and blank eyed
lifeless ragdolls in foaming cocoons
the sea already washing
them to a phosphorous nothing

I slide down the liquid shale
the bloody cull over
chains of wreckers take their plunder
up across the cliff leaving me alone
to piece back together limbs and souls
I wrap the dead in sacking
like butchers' best cuts of meat
hoisting their dismembered lives onto my back
and I begin my ascent on the path
to the pasture fields high above the sea

my hands, bloody with the grating gorse
its coconut scent catching in my throat
I drop my load on the muddied track
unexpectedly and violently heaving

my revulsion onto the purple sea drift
steadying myself against the churchyard wall
I wipe acidic lips on the back of my hand
the sweet smell of dung hanging in the air
opening the lychgate I place my cooling cargo
on to the low granite slab
recoiling as I hear the groan of dead flesh
loud against the dawn

HE LAY TWO SPARROWS

      at the doorstep   one for each
of the suns. Yes, there were still suns, even then. Yes,
there were still sparrows.   Called back to the labouring grass,
the men, the grass   which turned on the earth.
Like a bloodied horse   which turned on the earth,
the grass   he lay this too.
      She   a beret and tunic   waits in rumours
of sugar beets and oats   light like a great white snail
in her hair   waits in the forest of her echo. There he lay
two hills in the sparrows   one for each
of the worlds.
      He watched himself   as he was   a sparrow
on the doorstep   watched as he climbed one hill
and those who populated the hill before him
and built villages from cob and sparrow watched
as he lay worlds in the grass for the light.
      The gateway to the turning suns of the sparrows
the gateway to the hills of the sun.   Yes, there were still worlds,
yes, there was still a gate   at the gate   yes   still at the doorstep.

RETURNING EXCALIBUR

All at once, I have come to snow. This sword I must return
to you. To the lake I must   where you have been
rinsing music from midnight's skin, shaving the sky's oath
from stone. This sword   never mine
has carried weather   on its star metal face   could only carry
for so long could only carry   all my life   never mine
this weather   never mine   but this snow.

      And this chainmail of light   turned frost by moor
this light I return to you. All at once, night
has burnt itself low. Early this year, the kestrels
have fallen. No matter the infinite stirring
of sheep   floating language of tors. No matter.
I will find you in even this stirring   you
in the closing fissure of rock   in the water balancing
weather on its spears.   Even still.

      If this is night, there must be a lake.
There must be more lake than night. But snow.
Whatever you give I have returned
to you. All at once, I return to you.

Anthony Vahni Capildeo FRSL is a Trinidadian Scottish writer of poetry and non-fiction. Currently Professor and Writer in Residence at the University of York, their site-specific word and visual art includes responses to Cornwall's former capital, Launceston, as the Causley Trust Poet in Residence (2022) and to the Ubatuba granite of the Henry Moore Institute in Leeds (2023), as well as to Scottish, Irish, and Caribbean built and natural environments. A trustee at the Causley Trust they have numerous awards books and pamphlets including the Cholmondeley Award (Society of Authors) and the Forward Poetry Prize for Best Collection.

'Summer, Launceston' appeared in Anthony Vahni Capildeo,
Polkadot Wounds (Carcanet, 2024)

Sarah Cave is a poet, publisher and Steiner-Waldorf Class Guardian. She completed her PhD on the poetics of prayer at Royal Holloway last year. Her third collection, *The Book of Yona*, was published on Good Friday, 2024. As a publisher, she co-edits Guillemot Press with her husband Luke Thompson.

* Poems first published in *like fragile clay,*
(Guillemot Press, 2018)

Cahal Dallat was born in Ballycastle, County Antrim, and is a London-based poet, musician and critic. Cahal is founder/organiser of the *WB Yeats Bedford Park Project*, has won both *Strokestown International* and *Keats-Shelley* poetry prizes, and has recently been Charles Causley Centenary Writer/ Musician-in-Residence, Research Fellow at University of Texas, and joint Writer-in-Residence (with Anne-Marie Fyfe) at Lenoir-Rhyne University. His latest collection is *Beautiful Lofty Things*. www.cahaldallat.com

*Poems first published in *Beautiful Lofty Things,*
(Salmon Poetry, 2022)

David Devanny is an award-winning artist and poet, and Associate Professor in Multimedia Writing. He lives in Cornwall and works at Falmouth University. He writes page-based poetry and also makes digital poetry for exhibition spaces. In 2018 he was Writer in Residence at Cyprus Well, and he's now the Chair of the Charles Causley Trust.

US poet and critic **Dana Gioia** has published 6 poetry collections including *Interrogations at Noon* (American Book Award winner 2001), *99 Poems: New & Selected* (Poets' Prize winner 2016) and *Meet Me at the Lighthouse* (2023). He was Chairman of the National Endowment for the Arts and California State Poet Laureate - awarded the Laetare and Presidential Civilian Medals, and the Aiken-Taylor Award in Modern Poetry. www.danagioia.com

*"The Archbishop" first appeared in
Interrogations at Noon (Graywolf Press, 2001)

Alyson Hallett's latest publication is *End of the Glacier*, poems that respond to the paintings of Wilhelmina Barns-Graham. She is currently working on a book about listening to rocks and stones. Charles Causley continues to be an inspiration in Alyson's life: his passion, spirit and vision. http://www.alysonhallett.com

Aaron Kent is a working-class writer and insomniac from Cornwall. His 2nd poetry collection, *The Working Classic*, is available from the87press, and his debut, *Angels the Size of Houses*, is available from Shearsman. His poetry has been published by The Guardian, The BBC, and The Shakespeare Birthplace Trust among other places. He is an Arvon tutor, and his poetry has been translated into languages including French, Hungarian, German, Cymraeg, and Kernewek, and has been set to music.

Born in Liverpool in 1937, **Roger McGough** is the author of over 100 poetry books. During the sixties he was part of The Scaffold, whose song *Lily the Pink* became a worldwide hit, and wrote the ground-breaking collection *The Mersey Sound* (with Brian Patten and Adrian Henri) selling over a million copies. He is a Freeman of the City of Liverpool and in 2014 received the CBE for services to literature. He is the President of the Poetry Society and presents Poetry Please on BBC Radio 4.

*Published in the Causley at 70 publication,
copyright the Causley Trust

Andrew Motion was the UK Poet Laureate from 1999-2009 and was knighted for services to poetry in 1999. He is co-founder of the Poetry Archive, and since 2015 has lived in Baltimore, USA, where he is Homewood Professor of the Arts at Johns Hopkins University. His most recent collection is *New and Selected Poems* (Faber,2023).

Katrina Naomi is a poet, performer, mentor and judge. Her new collection, *Battery Rocks*, (Seren, 2024), has won the Arthur Welton Award. Katrina is a recipient of the Keats-Shelley Prize, Authors' Foundation and Saboteur Awards. Her poetry has appeared on Poems on the Underground, BBC Radio 4's *Front Row* and *Poetry Please*, in *The TLS*, *The Poetry Review* and *Modern Poetry in Translation*. She has a PhD from Goldsmiths and lives in Cornwall. www.katrinanaomi.co.uk

* Poems from *Battery Rocks* (Seren, 2024)

Originally from Lancashire and married to a Cornishman, **Nicola Nuttall** is the Director of the Causley Trust. She is a poet and cultural professional who studied on the Creative Writing Masters at Goldsmiths. She is currently undertaking a PhD at Falmouth University which will create a biography of the life and legacy of Charles Causley. Her poetry explores family, lived experience, deep time, and their interconnection with the natural world.

Judy O'Kane holds a PhD in Creative and Critical Writing from the University of East Anglia. Thirst, her non-fiction work-in-progress, was shortlisted for the Biographers' Club Tony Lothian Award. The judges described the work as 'a quest in many registers, and a celebration of the mystery of wine'. She has won the National Memory Day Prize, the Charles Causley Poetry Prize, the Irish Post Prize and the Listowel Writers' Week Original Poem Prize as well as prizes at Wells Festival of Literature, Guernsey Literary Festival, Glebe House, Enfield Poets and Kent and Sussex Poetry.

*'Olympia' and 'In Sibard's Well' first appeared in *Olympia* (*Clutag Press*, 2024)

Brian Patten is an English poet and author. He came to prominence in the 1960s as one of the Liverpool poets, alongside Adrian Henri and Roger McGough and writes primarily lyrical poetry about human relationships. His famous works include "Little Johnny's Confessions", "The Irrelevant Song", "Vanishing Trick", "Emma's Doll", and "Impossible Parents".

'Below Angel Hill' is an extract from a draft memoir and not for republication or use in print or on the internet.

Rachel Piercey writes for adults and for children. Her poems have appeared in magazines including *Bad Lilies, The Rialto, Butcher's Dog,* and *The Poetry Review*, and her most recent pamphlet, *Disappointing Alice*, was published by HappenStance. She runs *Tyger Tyger Magazine*, an online journal of new poems for children. In 2023, Rachel was the Causley Trust's poet in residence. rachelpierceypoet.com

*'Green Man' by Rachel Piercey was first published in *Gods and Monsters – Mythological Poems* (ed. Ana Sampson, Macmillan Children's Books, 2023).

Penelope Shuttle lives in Cornwall and is a founder member and President of the Falmouth Poetry Group. Until recently she was a Trustee of the Causley Trust. *Lyonesse,* her thirteenth collection (Bloodaxe Books, 2021) - was longlisted for the Laurel Prize. Recent publications include *Covid/Corvid* (*a* collaboration with Alyson Hallett), *Noah* (Broken Sleep Books, 2021 and 2023) and *History of the Child* (in preparation). Her poems can be heard on the Poetry Archive website. www.penelopeshuttle.co.uk

Rick Stein is a celebrity chef, restaurateur, writer and television presenter. Along with business partner Jill Stein, he runs the Stein hotel and restaurant business in the UK. He has received many awards for his work as a chef, teacher, presenter and author. He cooked twice for Tony Blair at 10 Downing Street, for the former French president Jacques Chirac and for Her Majesty the Queen and Prince Philip. In January 2003, Rick was awarded an OBE for services to West Country tourism.

Petrus (Peter) Ursem graduated in literature from the University of Utrecht and fine art from the Royal Academy, The Hague. He moved to England in 1998 and to Cornwall in 2011. To date he has published the 'Steven Honest' trilogy for YA readers and 'The Bigger Picture, Forty Friendly Fables' for older readers. He often incorporates poetry in his printworks. Until recently, Peter was the Development Manager at The Causley Trust.

Sue Wallace-Shaddad is digital writer-in-residence for the Charles Causley Trust's Literary Blog, *The Maker*. Sue is widely published and also writes poetry reviews and runs workshops. She has three published pamphlets *Sleeping Under Clouds* (Clayhanger Press 2023), *A City Waking Up* (Dempsey and Windle, 2020), and *Once There Was Colour* (Palewell Press, 2024). https://suewallaceshaddad.wordpress.com

    *'Tor' and 'It's the Little Things That Matter' were published by the Causley Trust as part of Sue's blogs for *The Maker*.

Tommy Sissons is a poet, novelist and playwright. He is the author of 'A Small Man's England' and 'Cautious, A Boat Adrift'. He arranged a poetry fundraiser in London in April 2024 and was a Poet in Residence at Cyprus Well, the longtime home of Charles Causley, in the summer of 2024.

    *published in a collection directly connected to Tommy's residency at Cyprus Well, by The Causley Trust

Rory Waterman's most recent collection is *Come Here to This Gate* (Carcanet, 2024). His first was a PBS Recommendation and was shortlisted for the Seamus Heaney Award and in 2019 he was shortlisted for the Ledbury Forte Prize. He was born in Belfast in 1981, grew up in Lincolnshire, and lives in Nottingham, where he teaches at NTU. rorywaterman.com.

> ***Carcanet have given f**ull approval for inclusion of Rory Waterman's poems in this publication.

Rowan Williams was Archbishop of Canterbury from 2002 to 2012, and Master of Magdalene College Cambridge from 2012 to 2020; he now lives in Wales. His Collected Poems appeared in 2021 (published by Carcanet) and an edited anthology, A Century of Poetry, in 2023 (SPCK).'

Born and raised in Hong Kong **Vera K Yuen**'s work has been featured in PN Review, The Lumiere Review and flipped eye. Previously, she was the winner of the 2022 Charles Causley International Poetry Competition and highly commended in the Disabled Poets Prize 2024. She is a Barbican Young Poet, keen mental health advocate and enjoys long walks in nature and solving crossword puzzles.

LAY OUT YOUR UNREST

www.ingramcontent.com/pod-product-compliance
Lightning Source LLC
Chambersburg PA
CBHW020212090426
42734CB00008B/1040